Short Like
HUMPTY DUMPTY

PAUL DOUGLAS CASTLE

STRATTON
—PRESS—
Publishing Life

Short Like Humpty Dumpty
Copyright © 2021 **Paul Douglas Castle**

Stratton Press Publishing
831 N Tatnall Street Suite M #188,
Wilmington, DE 19801
www.stratton-press.com
1-888-323-7009

ISBN (Paperback): 978-1-64895-562-4
ISBN (Ebook): 978-1-64895-563-1

Printed in the United States of America

Acknowledgements

IN ALL THE FOLLOWING STORIES, wherever scriptures appear, they are taken from the King James special study edition bible. The special study edition bible was published by the Global Bible Society at P.O. Box 6068, Ashville, NC 28816.

I thank them for the special bible they've published, and I do enjoy it extremely well. And everything else written in this book is my analogy, and it's based upon the word of God as I understand it. And I do want you to know, the word of God is the more excellent light in this world.

God bless you

Sincerely

Paul Douglas Castle

Bible story writer

Theologian of the heart

Creative story designer

Dedications

EVEN THOUGH THE NEEDED WORD of God isn't accepted by everyone, it's still available to all of us bible-savvy people interested in understanding the mysteries of our Great Creator God. However, it's up to us to dig deep and uncover His wonderful and unique mysteries.

Thanks to God, He's made sure we all have a chance to understand the reward of immortality and the consequences of damnation. And maybe He doesn't expect us seeking after Him to be as wise as theologians. However, maybe He does, and we should try and be as wise as theologians.

However, and which way it may be with our Great God, it doesn't hurt us to understand His important gospel extremely well. And mainly because, His gospel will improve our character by many folds. And I am warning you; men do perish for lack of bible knowledge.

I assure you; He's provided us enough information to understand the beginning of things until the end of things. And if we do not seek after understanding and the prize of immortality. Then our failure to grow wings and be similar to the angels is our fault.

I dedicate these bible stories to God first, then to my earthly father and mother, and Bryan Paul Castle, Aden Castle, Paul and Jason, and nephew David. My sincere love to all of them, and I do hope the best for you too.

Contents

Chapter One

HUMPTY DUMPTY

B EFORE THIS PARALLEL TO US story gets started, I do want you to know. Humpty Dumpty sat on a wall, content and happy until he had a great fall. Then all the king's daughters and all the king's men couldn't put Humpty Dumpty back together again.

This parallel to us story called *Humpty Dumpty* is a metaphor story, and it relates to a lot of relationships. And this means relationships between God and Lucifer, and us and God, and husbands and wives, and children and parents.

I am one hundred percent sure; Humpty Dumpty was a delicate old egg, well-traveled, well-dressed, and well-bred. He crossed the sea and traveled around the world, and there wasn't an egg as wise as him or frailer than him.

Humpty Dumpty was a vulnerable egg, concerned about his frailty. And he constantly worried about his shell, and he knew a fall would be the end of him. And the metaphor part of this story reveals, relationships are similar to a cracked eggshell.

Sometimes, our mood is serious. And sometimes, it's filled with laughter. And the first part of this story is humorous and funny, and it's easy to laugh at Humpty Dumpty. However, the rest of this story isn't so humous and funny, and it's much more serious than a cracked eggshell.

I do want you to know, the rest of this story entwines with a warning. And I am telling you, husbands and wives, mothers and daughters, fathers and sons. Beware, and do not crack the eggshell. Because sometimes, our relationships cannot be amended and put back together again.

This means stepping on toes gains us nothing but sore toes. And this truth means we better treat our relationships carefully and be cautious concerning all our decisions. And base everything we do on righteousness and fairness, or we'll take a great fall.

Characteristics of character matter, and so does the way we treat our fellow people. And all the king's daughters and all the king's men couldn't put Humpty Dumpty back together again. And this truth means, if we do too much harm to one another, our relationships will coincide with the end of Humpty Dumpty.

I hope you enjoy this metaphor story, designed especially to make us consider everything we do and say to all our friends and acquaintances and everyone else we meet along the way. And I do want you to know; we are our brother's keeper to some unknown degree.

Positively, this story isn't really about Humpty Dumpty, but it's about you and me and our actions and reactions, and considerations and inconsideration, and the consequences of our choices. And I do want to say, Humpty Dumpty was teaching the godly way before he fell off the wall.

In My Father's house are many mansions; I go to prepare a place for you!

Cruisin' above the clouds is expressing a Utopian metaphor, and it parallels to us reaching for the stars in the heavens above. And we are the cruisers, and the city of Utopia coincides with our hopes, dreams, and desires. However, it's somewhere above the clouds, and we'll have to become a spirit before we can find the city of Utopia.

Chapter Two

CRAZY

THIS AWARENESS STORY PARALLELING TO you and me, called crazy, is meant to shake our reality tree. And illuminate the sanity or the insanity of our spiritual condition. And I do want you to know, many of our choices in life parallel with our spiritual condition.

Positively and absolutely intentionally, this revealing story expands on the definition of crazy. And it adds the characteristics of our lifestyle to the definition of crazy, and it's extremely crazy to exhibit bad characteristics before the eyes of God.

This expansion of definition story means I am using the word crazy to illustrate bad decisions or rebellious decisions contrary to the required word of God. And whenever we put our gift of salvation in jeopardy, we are illuminating the definition of crazy.

The mainstream definition of crazy means not of sound mind, insane, unbalanced, and doing harmful things to ourselves that stable people wouldn't do. And when our spiritual condition becomes ungodly, and our prize of immortality is in jeopardy, then we fit the definition of crazy.

I want you to know for sure; being crazy means we've thrown caution to the wind. And we aren't careful enough, and we are doing potentially disastrous things we shouldn't be doing. And whenever we compromise the wonderful word of God, we are crazy.

Therefore, this concern for everyone alive story entwines a warning with the definition of crazy. And for everyone's sake, I am warning you and me and everyone else too. Please live cautiously because it's insane and dangerous to reject the required word of God.

Our wonderful and brilliant Creator God purposely gave us the perfect Ten Commandments. And they aren't optional if we desire to live in His kingdom. And this truth means it's insane and crazy to oppose His perfect and required Ten Commandments.

I do want you to realize; His perfect and infallible Ten Commandments are similar to having ten judges sitting on the bench in heaven. And every decision we make during our lifetime will be judged by the perfect Ten Commandments.

Which means the infallible Ten Commandments of God have great authority. And I do believe we should consider them a higher power, and it's crazy if we do not. And we would be wise to parallel them to ten judges.

Positively, the reality part of this story means sane decisions coincide with doing right. And the wonderful word of our Great Creator God assures us, all crazy decisions coincide with commandment breaking.

Supernatural abilities belong to our great Creator God, and he orchestrates all supernatural accomplishments. And you and I are monitored subjects living in a test ground world we do not fully understand.

I want you to know, Yehovah is our Great Supernatural Orchestrator God, and He's our designer of the right way. And please do understand, there's a price tag on sin, and He's the debt collector.

This means if we oppose His required word and erase His designed way of life from our conscience. Then it's highly probable; He'll orchestrate a reminder situation for our good. So, keep His wonderful commandments and dodge reminder situations.

This is our moment in time to set our destiny in concrete, and we better take advantage of this rare moment in time. And being a commandment-keeping Christian secures our future in the heavens above.

Chapter Three
GROWING INTO PERFECTION

BEYOND THE SHADOW OF A doubt, it was our wonderful God's responsibility to give us a road map to perfection. However, I do hope you realize; it's up to you and me to grow into perfection, and improve ourselves, day after day.

Purposely giving us a road map to perfection means our wonderful Creator God has great expectations of us. And I do want you to realize; He's prepping us for the next life. And He wouldn't give us a road map to perfection if He didn't love us.

I do want you to know, our wonderful Creator God desires for all believers in Christ to grow into perfection. And He wants us to become more similar to Christ, day after day. Until our degree of Christianity reaches one hundred percent.

Positively, every important decision we make in this life usually hinges on commandment-keeping. And His excellent and perfect Ten Commandments, infallible and superior, are the ultimate thing. And they have a say concerning whom gets the keys to heaven.

I am one hundred percent for sure; putting a difference between the holy and the unholy, and the clean and the unclean, and between right and wrong decisions illuminates our greatest challenge in this life.

Therefore, we can rise to the occasion, or we can forfeit our challenge. And we can wrongly believe the challenge to practice pure Christianity isn't essential. However, our challenge is important because we are taking a life and death test in the flesh.

Before this awareness story ends, I do hope and pray; you'll try to achieve the highest degree of Christianity. And you'll fall hopelessly in love with the perfect word of God, and you'll use authenticity to subtract compromises.

Conclusively, I want you to realize that the scale of one to ten is a metaphor mountain. And the closer we get to number ten means, we are conquering the metaphor mountain through the adherence of scripture authenticity.

This challenging story, challenging me and you, called growing into perfection. It entwines you and me to a higher degree of Christianity if we accept our challenge from our wonderful God. And I want you to realize, our Great Creator God is a challenging God.

When an angel from heaven opens the gates of hell, a loop of transformation is formed.

PAUL DOUGLAS CASTLE

Chapter Four

UNCARING CHILDREN

I ASSURE YOU, THERE ARE MANY uncaring children in this world, hard-hearted and unloving. And they will not honor, nor do they love or respect their father and mother. Still, yet, some of them pray many prayers to their Father in heaven.

However, these uncaring children do it without considering their behavior toward their parents that raised them from birth. And without considering the parallel of a father, they ask our great God for divine blessings and favor.

These cold-hearted children, as blind as a bat to their double standard, are uncaring. And sadly, to say, they haven't any respect for the parents that raised them. However, these insensitive children blindly expect their heavenly Father to respect them and help them.

Beyond the shadow of a doubt, close fellowship with their heavenly Father will be much harder for these kinds of hardhearted children to obtain. And sadly, to say, double standard children will be deceived by their imagination.

It's pretty obvious, these kinds of disobedient and hardhearted children, whom I am describing, have double standards. And mainly because they want to receive blessings from their heavenly Father. However, they bless not their father nor their mother on this earth.

I am one hundred percent certain; a child must be blind as a bat or as misguided as a ship without a compass. If they somehow believe their heavenly Father doesn't recognize mental cruelty to parents.

Therefore, I do want to declare a warning and tell all children of their parents. Children of disobedience, beware; our heavenly Father is watching and listening to you. And I do assure you, He's observing the way we treat our parents.

Furthermore, if we reap what we sow, and we usually do. Then not illustrating respect for our father and mother may result in recompense from our heavenly Father. And it's pretty possible; déjà vu may haunt us with our children.

Therefore, I advise you, children of parents, hate not the speck or flaw you see in your parent's character. And do not hold it against them if they aren't perfect. And mainly because, as the corridors of time pass by, you'll find out you have specks and flaws in your character too.

Furthermore, no one's perfect, and this analogy includes you and me. And do realize, the devil sifts us like wheat, and we are his victims of prey. And he'll sift the children of parents too, and no one escapes from his spirit torture.

The Fault of the Heart Book

The fault of the heart story places our heart in control of the things we do. And this means our desire to learn about God, or our failure to learn about our Creator God is a good quality of character, or it's a fault of the heart.

Beyond the shadow of a doubt, the heart has many faults, and we humans make mistakes all the time. However, regardless of the flaws of our hearts, the Incredible Holy Ghost of God is always trying to mend our faults.

Therefore, I do want you to realize, as time goes by, the heart will grow stronger in our great God. And our heart will become purer, or the faults of our heart will be too many to repair.

Salvation Formula

If thou shalt confess with thy mouth the Lord is Jesus, and shalt believe in thy heart that God the Father hath raised Him; Jesus Christ from the dead, then thou shalt be saved. For with the heart, man believeth unto righteousness: and with the mouth, confession is made unto salvation.

The Conclusion to the whole matter analogy

Reverence God and keep His commandments, for this is the whole duty of man. And I do want you to know, the gospel of God is the image of God. And the better we know His gospel, then the better we'll know Him.

Gathering at the well

In the days of old, there wasn't running water in the houses. And everyone gathered at the location of the well and filled their containers.

The wonderful and weary Son of God sat near the well one day, probably similar to this one. And a Samaritan woman gave Him water to drink, and in return, Yeshua offered her living water.

The living water Yeshua offered her; He offers to everyone willing to believe in Him and drink from the well that never runs dry. And Yeshua said to the woman at the well, I that speak to thee am He.

Chapter Five

ENTERTAINING STRANGERS

I KNOW FOR SURE; THE WONDERFUL Son of God is supernatural, and the power of transformation is artwork for Him. And this means race, gender, or color are immaterial if He decides to talk to you and me like a stranger on this earth.

Yeshua, the wonderful Son of God, and His loyal apostles were journeying toward the temple of Herod. And people everywhere along the way were excited, and they were glad to see the wonderful Son of God pass by.

Bible scriptures reveal the goodness and mercy of Jesus proceeded Him, where so ever He traveled on this earth. And recorded events show many people believed in the wonderful Son of God with all their heart, and I do too.

Beyond the shadow of a doubt, His reputation went before Him, similar to a wildfire spreading fast through dry grass in strong winds. And His reputation on this earth was good and similar to that of an innocent lamb.

Definitely, bible scriptures reveal, He looked just like other men. And the wonderful Son of God proceeded through life eating and drinking and sleeping, the same way all other flesh and blood men do.

However, His super intelligence and His supernatural abilities were superior to all other men. And His many miracles and His unlimited mercy toward humble people separated Him from other men. And someday, we'll know Him personally.

Furthermore, the corridors of time haven't any restrictions concerning His ability to walk among men undetected. And the unknown author responsible for giving us the wonderful book of Hebrews said, Be not forgetful to entertain strangers.

Hebrew 13:2 For thereby some have entertained <u>angels</u> (means heavenly angels) unaware.

This means you and I could also entertain the Son of God unaware and not realize it's Him we are talking to at the moment. And mainly because, The Son of God can look like other men. And, I am sure, He visits every generation of people living on this earth.

Honestly, I do hope and pray, for the sake of preserving your soul, you'll meet the wonderful Son of God someday. And you'll become a loyal son, or a loyal daughter to Him, and be a happy resident in the peaceful kingdom of God.

Chapter Six

THE GRAND CANYON

THIS EXPOSURE STORY CALLED *The Grand Canyon* isn't really about the incredible Grand Canyon in Arizona. However, this story does reveal another Canyon, and it's impossible to cross. And sometimes, men and women get stranded on the wrong side of the canyon.

The truthful word of God assures us; there's a division between two opposing seeds. And the corridors of time prove both seeds will never see things the same way. And for this reason, there will come a separation day in the future, and the wheat and the tares will be separated from each other.

Furthermore, the favored by God prophet called Abraham. He clearly tells us, so we'll know for sure. There's a tremendous fixed gulf between the kingdom of God and the kingdom of Lucifer, and no man can cross over it.

This next awareness scripture is absolutely clear, and it's told by the wonderful Son of God. And this following scripture illuminates the great gulf, designed to divide the good seed from the bad seed, or better said, the godly person from the ungodly person.

The great gulf divides two kingdoms from each other, and it isn't any different than building a high wall between good and evil. Only the great gulf no man can cross exceeds the security of a high wall. Simply because our great Creator God built the great gulf.

Luke 16:26 And besides all this, between <u>us</u> (Abraham and Lazarus) and <u>you</u> (corrupt rich man) there is a great gulf fixed so that they which would <u>pass</u> (means cross) from <u>hence</u> (heaven) to you cannot;

Luke 16:26 Neither can <u>they</u> (the bad seed) pass to <u>us</u> (the good seed) that would come from <u>thence</u> (from the realms of hell).

As far as I know, the bad seed began with the wicked and murderous Cain, and Cain was the first-born son of Lucifer and Eve. And there's not any bible evidence pointing to any other time and place of his origin.

The wicked Lucifer is also known as the serpent of old, and the war god, and the tree of knowledge of good and evil. And the demonic Lucifer is the abomination of desolation, regardless of wherever he stands, and he will destroy whosoever he can.

I assure you; the wicked Lucifer is the blind guide from the heavens above, and the blind follow the blind. And the great gulf, somewhat similar to the Grand Canyon, separates the spiritually blind person from the believers in Christ.

Chapter Seven

I'LL REMEMBER YOU

THIS INFORMATIVE STORY BASED ON the words of Yeshua, called *I'll remember you*. It entwines you and me and God together if we are a believer in Christ. And if we do not believe in Christ, then we'll not be invited to live in His wonderful kingdom.

The phrase saying, I'll remember you is built on mutual love, and mutual love means we cannot forget about being loyal to our wonderful Creator God. And not forgetting to be loyal means, He'll not forget us whenever we call on His name.

This remembrance story, called I'll remember you, is built on rock-solid sincere love, and genuine love is the right ingredient, designed to make believers strong in the perfect word of God. And the phrase saying, I'll remember you are words intended for the disciples of Christ.

We may be ordinary and average people, and we may not set the world on fire. However, we can be friends with a strong God, and being friends with Him makes us special people. And I do want you to know, sincere believers in Him are called the disciples of Christ.

You and I may not have the authority to do supernatural works in the name of the Lord, the same way Elijah did and Moses did. However, we can be good servants to God through ordinary and everyday works. And all we do; we can do for the glory of God.

Positively, good works done for the glory of God pleases our wonderful Creator God the most. And it should be our pleasure to honor our great God, and when we lift up Yehovah through loyalty to Him.

Then our name and our good works will not be forgotten in our time of need. However, I do sincerely advise you and warn you too. It would be wise to find our wonderful and merciful God before our time of need arrives.

Just knowing this important fact alone should inspire a person to hunger for the wonderful word of God and consider His word every time our heart-beats. And if we do, He'll remember us. And the phrase called I'll remember you means; God is watching us from above. And He will remember our loyalty to Him every time His heartbeats.

The above picture is a front cover picture on one of my books called *No Favorites*. However, at a later time, I wrote another book called *Sifting the Wheat*. Anyway, the book called *No Favorites* also exposes the wheat sifter.

Sifting the wheat is symbolic of us, and sifting the wheat is Lucifer's favorite game. And I am one hundred percent for sure; Lucifer sifts the wheat, day after day. And when he finds vulnerable prey, he sifts them like wheat.

No Favorites Analogy

The analogy of no favorites reveals the perfect fairness of God. And no favorites mean all of us are judged on our own merits. And even though, we live among millions of people, our exhibition of merits profile us as an individual.

No favorites mean all of us are treated equally by our Supreme God. And certain people will not be exempt for the ungodly things other people are disciplined for doing. And no favorites mean the expectations of God are the same for everyone since He doesn't discriminate between race, gender, or color.

Self-Examination Analogy

Beyond the shadow of a doubt, we can all agree, none of us are perfect. And I am one hundred percent sure; we cannot say we do not need a periotic self-examination. And as sure as the moon comes up every night, we all need a periotic self-examination.

I assure you; if we care about improving our image, a self-examination is good for us. And a self-examination will improve our character by many folds if we can detect our faults and are willing to fix our flaws.

The Eye of the needle metaphor

Within this serious picture, *The Eye of the Needle* doesn't represent rich men only. And we would be foolish to believe, the Eye of the needle doesn't include everyone. Simply because the Eye of the needle doesn't discriminate, and it does include everyone and every sin.

Chapter Eight

THE EYE OF THE NEEDLE

THE EYE OF THE NEEDLE is symbolic of a two-edged sword and sharper than the sharpest razor. It's a metaphor story, and it hovers between the literal and the symbolic, similar to a ghost guarding angel. And the Eye of the needle discerns the godly from the ungodly.

The Eye of the needle is never wrong, and it distinguishes between the hot and the cold and the lukewarm. And the temperature of our love for God must be hot before we can get through the Eye of the needle.

The Eye of the needle is infallible and honest to the highest degree. And it doesn't recognize race, color, or gender. However, the Eye of the needle does see through the exterior of the flesh, and it looks deep inside the heart.

The Eye of the needle has great power, and it entwines with the word of God, and it's been around since the beginning of time. And it established itself from the Ancient of Days, and the Eye of the needle has an immortal lifespan.

The Eye of the needle entwines with the Father, and the Son, and the Holy Ghost. And the righteous Eye of the needle has roots to every living thing, and every living thing with a brain will stand before the Eye of the needle someday.

In the Ancient of Days, equal rights weren't as complicated as they are now. However, I do want everyone to know, the Eye of the needle distinguishes between necessary equal rights and fabricated equal rights.

The brilliant Eye of the needle never makes a mistake, and it always puts godliness and righteousness first. And regardless of who we are or the color of our skin, or the outward appearance of our image, godliness is the characteristic that matters the most to the Eye of the needle.

Positively, the righteous Eye of the needle is choosy, and certain things do matter to the Eye of the needle. And because of its pre-design, it doesn't allow ungodliness and unrighteousness to pass through its narrow filtering process of scrutiny.

The never wrong Eye of the needle has power over life and death. And I do want you to know in advance, passing through the Eye of the needle extends life, and not getting through the Eye of the needle means certain death.

Conclusively, I do want you to realize, the Eye of the needle is strong enough to enforce the will of our Great Creator God, and the Eye of the needle keeps out the camels. And it lets through the sheep, and there are no exceptions to this rule.

Walking on Water

After the wonderful Son of God heard distressing news, declaring that John the Baptist was beheaded, Yeshua departed by ship to a desert place. And when the people heard of His going, they followed Him.

The wonderful Son of God was overwhelmed with compassion for the multitudes, and He healed their sick. And He fed five thousand men and women with *two fishes* and *five loaves of bread.*

Afterward, His ship departed without Him, and it was a long way from the shoreline. And the scriptures reveal, our incredible Son of God walked on water to join His friends on the ship.

Chapter Nine

POINT BLANK

OMETIMES, A MESSAGE IS SO extremely important; it needs to be told point-blank with absolute unquivering truth. And this is one of those important stories, and for the sake of saving lost souls, I am going to tell you this story point-blank.

Positively, you and I can ask ourselves, and we can ponder the unknown question. How many words will it take before some men and women figure out how to achieve eternal life? And I do advise you, learn all you can about our Creator God.

The wonderful Son of God told us point blank the way to achieve eternal life when He said. I am the way, the truth, and eternal life, and no man cometh unto the Father, but by Me. And we do have to get by Him before we receive the gift of immortality.

Conclusively, this concerning story is asking you how many words will it take. Before you hate ungodliness, and give yourself entirely to the wonderful

Son of God and become a red-hot Christian. And we will have to be a commandment-lover before we can get by Him.

Please be aware, as we endeavor to become a red-hot Christian, we have a powerful and evil adversary called the wicked Lucifer. And I am one hundred percent sure; Lucifer wants us to be a lukewarm or arctic cold unbeliever.

Positively, I do guarantee you; the wicked Lucifer doesn't want us to be hot and on fire for the needed and wonderful word of God. And it's because he hates God lovers and all hot and on fire Christians.

I assure you; almost all the people in this world have a temperature malfunction or a burnt-out heating element gone bad within the center of their heart. And for an illogical reason surpassing good sense, their heat will not increase for the love of God.

It's for this reason, I do wonder, how many words will it take to restore the heat they need before they can be hot and on fire for the wonderful word of God? And I do warn you; it takes heat to get through the pearl gates in heaven.

Positively, on Judgment Day, seriously important to everyone. It'll be much better to face God as a red-hot Christian rather than a lukewarm or cold person. And this story called point blank is saying, keep the fire burning hot.

On the wings of a snow-white dove, our great God sent down His pure sweet love. And this is another way of saying, He sent His Son to us.

A Savior is born in the flesh, and saying happy birthday pleases Him much. Amen, Amen, Amen. And even though the date of His birth is a controversial subject, and the hour and the day is a mystery, no man can say for sure.

However, I do want you to realize, the day and the hour aren't really important to know. However, we must remember Him, and I am glad for the privilege to say Happy Birthday to the Son of God.

Chapter Ten

THE DOOR

T HIS SERIOUSLY IMPORTANT SHORT STORY called the door only has one purpose of achieving. And it's an educational purpose meant to reveal the formula for gaining immortality. And if we are wise enough to do the will of our great God, we'll be invited to walk through the door.

This is a straight-up and serious story, and it's meant to contradict the many false formulas circulating among unlearned people. And this following informative scripture reveals the only door to salvation. And it portrays the other side of the door as a peaceful place to rest.

John 10:9 Jesus says, I am the <u>door</u> (to salvation and the truth): By Me, if any man enters in, he shall be saved and shall go out and find <u>pasture</u> (means find a peaceful place to rest).

The rock-solid word of God assures us, there is only one door all men and women can enter through if they want to find eternal salvation and find the

Utopian place where the immortals live. And for this reason, we better search for the door until we find it.

Furthermore, the wonderful Son of God is the gatekeeper, and He opens and closes, and admits and rejects, who so ever He chooses to allow entry or refuse entry. And for our sake, we better fall in love with His commanded word and secure our name on the invitation list.

Positively, I do want you to know, our high degree of love for Him is the admission ticket to the other side. And I also want you to know, not loving the Son of God and not loving His word means no admission through the door.

Conclusively, myths and fairy tales and conjured up beliefs availeth nothing. However, I do testify, finding the wonderful Son of God means we've found the right door. And finding the right door means we've discovered a great pearl in this world, and we never want to part with it. And when our time comes to leave this world, the gatekeeper will open the door for you and me.

Filthy Rags Analogy

My definition of filthy rags illuminates the inability to be perfect, even while trying to be perfect, but falling short. However, my definition of ungodly filthy rags portrays evil and ungodly men going beyond the boundaries of falling short.

Therefore, I do sincerely conclude; there's a moral boundary line drawn between filthy rags and ungodly filthy rags. And I do want you to realize; the penalty is greater when we cross the boundary line.

This analogy means we would be wrong to believe one person is as filthy as another. And so, the scripture in Isaiah, saying, all our righteousness is as filthy rags. It doesn't mean there isn't a dividing point separating filthy rags from ungodly filthy rags. And none of us are perfect, but we aren't equally filthy.

Synopsis

THIS INCREDIBLE BOOK CALLED SHORT like Humpty Dumpty is saying, this book is completely written with short stories. And it's simply designed for waiting rooms and office rooms where reading time is short. And for everyone's pleasure, all the stories in this book are gentle reading material.

All the stories in this book are written in number sixteen font, purposely designed to make reading easier for all age groups. And especially for young boys and girls, the older ladies and gentlemen, or anyone having impaired vision.

Some of the beautiful pictures in this book, outstanding and incredible, are hand-drawn by an amazing unknown artist. And maybe she was as good as Leonardo da Vinci, or Raphael, or Vincent van Gogh. And for the benefit of satisfying curiosity, this book gives every reader a sample of her ability to create beautiful artwork.

The famous Mona Lisa cannot compare to the beauty of the pictures and stories this book represents. Since things that represent our great God in all His glory illustrates the highest degree of beauty. And I do want you to know, revealing God to this world through meaningful stories is a beautiful form of artwork.

This short storybook and its beautiful pictures are designed to illuminate God to the uttermost degree of recognition. And the creation of these individual stories is my way of lifting Him higher than the stars in the sky. And the analogy of this book concludes the word of God is the pinnacle of our greatest needs.

CPSIA information can be obtained
at www.ICGtesting.com
Printed in the USA
BVHW050942221121
622229BV00015B/491